DONNA GREEN

LEAVES FROM

A CHILD'S GARDEN OF VERSES

ROBERT LOUIS STEVENSON
Illustrated by Donna Green

SMITHMARK

This edition first published in 1992 by SMITHMARK
16 East 32nd Street, New York, NY 10016

SMITHMARK books are available for bulk purchase for sales promotions and premium use. For details write or telephone the manager of special sales, SMITHMARK Publishers, Inc., 16 East 32nd Street, New York, NY 10016; (212) 532-6600

Produced by VIA
℅ Vermilion
P.O. Box 176,
Cohasset, MA 02025

A Rob Fremont Book

Design by Carol Belanger Grafton
Editor: Victoria Fremont
Composition: Trufont Typographers, Inc.

Decorative silhouettes reprinted by permission of
Dover Publications, Inc. New York, NY

ISBN: 0-8317-5697-7

Printed and bound in Singapore by Imago Publishing

10 9 8 7 6 5 4

FOR MONIQUE
AND ADAM

CONTENTS

TIME TO RISE / 10

A THOUGHT / 11

THE WIND / 12

THE SWING / 13

THE SUN'S TRAVELS / 14

SINGING / 16

RAIN / 17

MY KINGDOM / 18

HAPPY THOUGHT / 19

THE MOON / 20

FROM A RAILWAY CARRIAGE / 21

A GOOD BOY / 22

PIRATE STORY / 24

FOREIGN LANDS / 25

TRAVEL / 26

A GOOD PLAY / 28

THE LAND OF COUNTERPANE / 29

MY SHIP AND I / 30

MY SHADOW / 32

FAIRY BREAD / 33

THE UNSEEN PLAYMATE / 34

MARCHING SONG / 36

ARMIES IN THE FIRE / 37

BLOCK CITY / 38

MY BED IS A BOAT / 40

THE LAND OF STORYBOOKS / 41

THE FLOWERS / 42

WHERE GO THE BOATS? / 44

THE GARDENER / 45

SUMMER SUN / 46

AT THE SEASIDE / 47

THE COW / 48

THE HAYLOFT / 49

FAREWELL TO THE FARM / 50

AUTUMN FIRES / 52

ESCAPE AT BEDTIME / 53

PICTURE-BOOKS IN WINTER / 54

WINDY NIGHTS / 56

BED IN SUMMER / 57

WINTERTIME / 58

NIGHT AND DAY / 60

KEEPSAKE MILL / 62

MY TREASURES / 64

LOOKING FORWARD / 65

TO WILLIE AND HENRIETTA / 66

YOUNG NIGHT THOUGHT / 68

THE LAND OF NOD / 69

TO MY MOTHER / 70

NORTH-WEST PASSAGE / 72

TO ANY READER / 74

FIRST LINE INDEX / 76

TIME TO RISE

A birdie with a yellow bill
Hopped upon the window sill,
Cocked his shining eye and said:
"Ain't you 'shamed, you sleepyhead?"

A THOUGHT

*I*t is very nice to think
The world is full of meat and drink,
With little children saying grace
In every Christian kind of place.

THE SUN'S TRAVELS

The sun is not a-bed, when I
At night upon my pillow lie;
Still round the earth his way he takes,
And morning after morning makes.

While here at home, in shining day,
We round the sunny garden play,
Each little Indian sleepyhead
Is being kissed and put to bed.

And when at eve I rise from tea,
Day dawns beyond the Atlantic Sea,
And all the children in the West
Are getting up and being dressed.

SINGING

Of speckled eggs the birdie sings
And nests among the trees;
The sailor sings of ropes and things
In ships upon the seas.

The children sing in far Japan,
The children sing in Spain;
The organ with the organ man
Is singing in the rain.

RAIN

The rain is raining all around,
It falls on field and tree,
It rains on the umbrellas here,
And on the ships at sea.

MY KINGDOM

Down by a shining water well
I found a very little dell,
No higher than my head.
The heather and the gorse about
In summer bloom were coming out,
Some yellow and some red.

I called a little pool a sea;
The little hills were big to me,
For I am very small.
I made a boat, I made a town,
I searched the caverns up and down,
And named them one and all.

And all about was mine, I said,
The little sparrows overhead,
The little minnows too.
This was the world and I was king;
For me the bees came by to sing,
For me the swallows flew.

I played there were no deeper seas,
Nor any wider plains than these,
Nor other kings than me.
At last I heard my mother call
Out from the house at evenfall,
To call me home to tea.

And I must rise and leave my dell,
And leave my dimpled water well,
And leave my heather blooms.
Alas! and as my home I neared,
How very big my nurse appeared,
How great and cool the rooms!

HAPPY THOUGHT

The world is so full of a number of things,
I'm sure we should all be as happy as kings.

A GOOD BOY

I woke before the morning, I was happy all the day.
I never said an ugly word, but smiled and stuck to play.

And now at last the sun is going down behind the wood,
And I am very happy, for I know that I've been good.

My bed is waiting cool and fresh, with linen smooth and fair,
And I must be off to sleepsin-by, and not forget my prayer.

I know that, till tomorrow I shall see the sun arise,
No ugly dream shall fright my mind, no ugly sight my eyes.

But slumber hold me tightly till I waken in the dawn,
And hear the thrushes singing in the lilacs round the lawn.

PIRATE STORY

Three of us afloat in the meadow by the swing,
Three of us aboard in the basket on the lea.
Winds are in the air, they are blowing in the spring,
And waves are on the meadow like the waves there are at sea.

Where shall we adventure, today that we're afloat,
Wary of the weather and steering by a star?
Shall it be to Africa, a-steering of the boat,
To Providence, or Babylon, or off to Malabar?

Hi! but here's a squadron a-rowing on the sea—
Cattle on the meadow a-charging with a roar!
Quick, and we'll escape them, they're as mad as they can be,
The wicket is the harbor and the garden is the shore.

FOREIGN LANDS

Up into the cherry tree
Who should climb but little me?
I held the trunk with both my hands
And looked abroad on foreign lands.

I saw the next door garden lie,
Adorned with flowers before my eye,
And many pleasant places more
That I had never seen before.

I saw the dimpling river pass
And be the sky's blue looking-glass;
The dusty roads go up and down
With people tramping in to town.

If I could find a higher tree,
Farther and farther I should see,
To where the grown up river slips
Into the sea among the ships.

To where the roads on either hand
Lead onward into fairy land,
Where all the children dine at five,
And all the playthings come alive.

TRAVEL

I should like to rise and go
Where the golden apples grow—
Where below another sky
Parrot islands anchored lie,
And, watched by cockatoos and goats,
Lonely Crusoes building boats—
Where in sunshine reaching out
Eastern cities, miles about,
Are with mosque and minaret
Among sandy gardens set,
And the rich goods from near and far
Hang for sale in the bazaar—
Where the Great Wall round China goes,
And on one side the desert blows,
And with bell and voice and drum,
Cities on the other hum—
Where are forests, hot as fire,
Wide as England, tall as a spire,
Full of apes and coconuts
And the negro hunters' huts—

Where the knotty crocodile
Lies and blinks in the Nile,
And the red flamingo flies
Hunting fish before his eyes—
Where in jungles, near and far,
Man-devouring tigers are,
Lying close and giving ear
Lest the hunt be drawing near,
Or a comer-by be seen
Swinging in a palanquin—
Where among the desert sands
Some deserted city stands,
All its children, sweep and prince,
Grown to manhood ages since,
Not a foot in street or house,
Not a stir of child or mouse,
And when kindly falls the night,
In all the town no spark of light.
There I'll come when I'm a man
With a camel caravan;
Light a fire in the gloom
Of some dusty dining room;
See the pictures on the walls,
Heroes, fights and festivals;
And in a corner find the toys
Of the old Egyptian boys.

MY SHADOW

I have a little shadow that goes in and out with me,
And what can be the use of him is more than I can see.
He is very, very like me from the heels up to the head;
And I see him jump before me, when I jump into my bed.

The funniest thing about him is the way he likes to grow—
Not at all like proper children, which is always very slow;
For he sometimes shoots up taller like an india-rubber ball,
And he sometimes gets so little that there's none of him at all.

He hasn't got a notion of how children ought to play,
And can only make a fool of me in every sort of way.
He stays so close beside me, he's a coward you can see;
I'd think shame to stick to nursie as that shadow sticks to me!

One morning very early, before the sun was up,
I rose and found the shining dew on every buttercup;
But my lazy little shadow, like an arrant sleepy-head,
Had stayed at home behind me and was fast asleep in bed.

FAIRY BREAD

Come up here, O dusty feet!
Here is fairy bread to eat.
Here in my retiring room,
Children, you may dine
On the golden smell of broom
And the shade of pine;
And when you have eaten well,
Fairy stories hear and tell.

THE UNSEEN PLAYMATE

When children are playing alone on the green,
In comes the playmate that never was seen.
When children are happy and lonely and good,
The Friend of the Children comes out of the wood.

Nobody heard him and nobody saw,
His is a picture you never could draw,
But he's sure to be present, abroad or at home,
When children are happy and playing alone.

He lies in the laurels, he runs on the grass,
He sings when you tinkle the musical glass;
Whene'er you are happy and cannot tell why,
The Friend of the Children is sure to be by!

He loves to be little, he hates to be big,
'Tis he that inhabits the caves that you dig;
'Tis he when you play with your soldiers of tin
That sides with the Frenchmen and never can win.

'Tis he when at night you go off to your bed,
Bids you go to your sleep and not trouble your head;
For wherever they're lying, in cupboard or shelf,
'Tis he will take care or your playthings himself!

MARCHING SONG

Bring the comb and play upon it!
Marching, here we come!
Willie cocks his highland bonnet,
Johnnie beats the drum.

Mary Jane commands the party,
Peter leads the rear;
Feet in time, alert and hearty,
Each a Grenadier!

All in the most martial manner
Marching double-quick;
While the napkin like a banner
Waves upon the stick!

Here's enough of fame and pillage,
Great commander Jane!
Now that we've been round the village,
Let's go home again.

The lamps now glitter down the street;
Faintly sound the falling feet;
And the blue even slowly falls
About the garden trees and walls.

Now in the falling of the gloom
The red fire paints the empty room;
And warmly on the roof it looks,
And flickers on the backs of books.

Armies march by tower and spire
Of cities blazing, in the fire—
Till as I gaze with staring eyes,
The armies fade, the luster dies.

Then once again the glow returns;
Again the phantom city burns;
And down the red-hot valley, lo!
The phantom armies marching go!

Blinking embers, tell me true,
Where are those armies marching to,
And what the burning city is
That crumbles in your furnaces!

BLOCK CITY

What are you able to build with your blocks?
Castles and palaces, temples and docks.
Rain may keep raining, and others go roam,
But I can be happy and building at home.

Let the sofa be mountains, the carpet be sea,
There I'll establish a city for me:
A kirk and a mill and a palace beside,
And a harbor as well where my vessels may ride.

Great is the palace with pillar and wall,
A sort of a tower on the top of it all,
And steps coming down in an orderly way,
To where my toy vessels lie safe in the bay.

This one is sailing and that one is moored;
Hark to the song of the sailors on board!
And see, on the steps of my palace, the kings
Coming and going with presents and things!

Now I have done with it, down let it go!
All in a moment the town is laid low.
Block upon block lying scattered and free,
What is there left of my town by the sea?

Yet as I saw it, I see it again,
The kirk and the palace, the ships and the men,
And as long as I live and where'er I may be,
I'll always remember my town by the sea.

MY BED IS A BOAT

My bed is like a little boat;
Nurse helps me in when I embark;
She girds me in my sailor's coat
And starts me in the dark.

At night I go on board and say
Good-night to all my friends on shore:
I shut my eyes and sail away
And see and hear no more.

And sometimes things to bed I take,
As prudent sailors have to do:
Perhaps a slice of wedding cake,
Perhaps a toy or two.

All night across the dark we steer;
But when the day returns at last,
Safe in my room beside the pier,
I find my vessel fast.

THE LAND OF STORYBOOKS

At evening when the lamp is lit,
Around the fire my parents sit;
They sit at home and talk and sing,
And do not play at anything.

Now, with my little gun, I crawl
All in the dark along the wall,
And follow round the forest track
Away behind the sofa back.

There, in the night, where none can spy,
All in my hunter's camp I lie,
And play at books that I have read
Till it is time to go to bed.

These are the hills, there are the woods,
These are my starry solitudes;
And there the river by whose brink
The roaring lions come to drink.

I see the others far away
As if in firelit camp they lay,
And I, like to an Indian scout,
Around their party prowled about.

So, when my nurse comes in for me,
Home I return across the sea,
And go to bed with backward looks
At my dear land of Storybooks.

THE FLOWERS

*A*ll the names I know from nurse:
Gardener's garters, Shepherd's purse,
Bachelor's buttons, Lady's smock,
And the Lady Hollyhock.
Fairy places, fairy things,
Fairy woods where the wild bee wings,
Tiny trees for tiny dames—
These must all be fairy names!

Tiny woods below whose boughs
Shady fairies weave a house;
Tiny tree tops, rose or thyme,
Where the braver fairies climb!

Fair are grown-up people's trees,
But the fairest woods are these,
Where, if I were not so tall,
I should live for good and all.

SUMMER SUN

Great is the sun, and wide he goes
    Through empty heaven without repose;
And in the blue and glowing days
More thick than rain he showers his rays.

Though closer still the blinds we pull
To keep the shady parlor cool,
Yet he will find a chink or two
To slip his golden fingers through.

The dusty attic spider-clad
He, through the keyhole, maketh glad;
And through the broken edge of tiles,
Into the laddered hayloft smiles.

Meantime his golden face around
He bares to all the garden ground,
And sheds a warm and glittering look
Among the ivy's inmost nook.

Above the hills, along the blue,
Round the bright air with footing true,
To please the child, to paint the rose,
The gardener of the World, he goes.

AT THE SEASIDE

When I was down beside the sea
A wooden spade they gave to me
To dig the sandy shore.

My holes were empty like a cup,
In every hole the sea came up,
Till it could come no more.

FAREWELL TO THE FARM

The coach is at the door at last;
The eager children, mounting fast
And kissing hands, in chorus sing:
Good-bye, good-bye, to everything!

To house and garden, field and lawn,
The meadow-gates we swang upon,
To pump and stable, tree and swing,
Good-bye, good-bye, to everything!

And fare you well for evermore,
O ladder at the hayloft door,
O hayloft where the cobwebs cling,
Good-bye, good-bye, to everything!

Crack goes the whip, and off we go;
The trees and houses smaller grow;
Last, round the woody turn we swing:
Good-bye, good-bye, to everything!

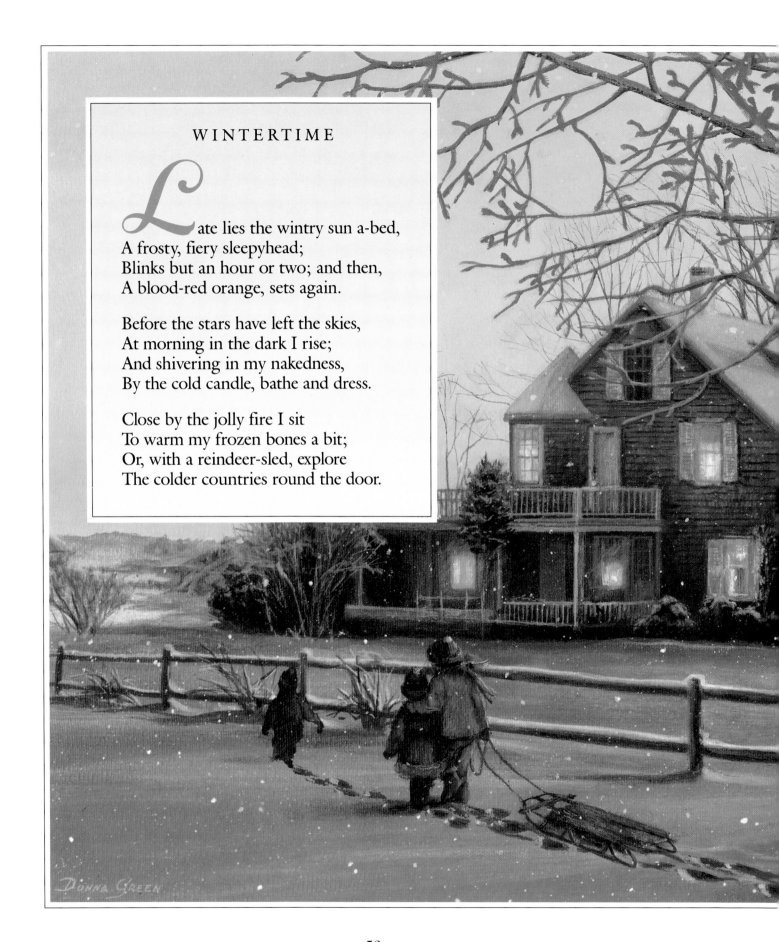

WINTERTIME

Late lies the wintry sun a-bed,
A frosty, fiery sleepyhead;
Blinks but an hour or two; and then,
A blood-red orange, sets again.

Before the stars have left the skies,
At morning in the dark I rise;
And shivering in my nakedness,
By the cold candle, bathe and dress.

Close by the jolly fire I sit
To warm my frozen bones a bit;
Or, with a reindeer-sled, explore
The colder countries round the door.

When to go out, my nurse doth wrap
Me in my comforter and cap,
The cold wind burns my face, and blows
Its frosty pepper up my nose.

Black are my steps on silver sod,
Thick blows my frosty breath abroad;
And tree and house, and hill and lake,
Are frosted like a wedding cake.

MY TREASURES

*T*hese nuts, that I keep in the back of the nest,
Where all my lead soldiers are lying at rest,
Were gathered in autumn by nursie and me
In a wood with a well by the side of the sea.

This whistle we made (and how clearly it sounds!)
By the side of a field at the end of the grounds.
Of a branch of a plane, with a knife of my own,
It was nursie who made it, and nursie alone!

The stone, with the white and the yellow and grey,
We discovered I cannot tell how far away;
And I carried it back, although weary and cold,
For though father denies it, I'm sure it is gold.

But of all my treasures the last is the king,
For there's very few children possess such a thing;
And that is a chisel, both handle and blade,
Which a man who was really a carpenter made.

LOOKING FORWARD

When I am grown to man's estate
I shall be very proud and great,
And tell the other girls and boys
Not to meddle with my toys.

TO WILLIE AND HENRIETTA

If two may read aright
These rhymes of old delight
And house and garden play,
You two, my cousins, and you only, may

You in a garden green
With me were king and queen,
Were hunter, soldier, tar,
And all the thousand things that children are.

Now in the elders' seat
We rest with quiet feet,
And from the window-bay
We watch the children, our successors, play.

"Time was," the golden head
Irrevocably said;
But time which none can bind,
While flowing fast away, leaves love behind.

TO MY MOTHER

You too, my mother, read my rhymes
For love of unforgotten times,
And you may chance to hear once more
The little feet along the floor.

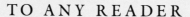

TO ANY READER

As from the house your mother sees
You playing round the garden trees,
So you may see, if you will look
Through the windows of this book,
Another child, far, far away,
And in another garden, play.
But do not think you can at all,
By knocking on the window, call
That child to hear you. He intent
Is all on his play-business bent.

He does not hear; he will not look,
Nor yet be lured out of this book.
For, long ago, the truth to say,
He has grown up and gone away,
And it is but a child of air
That lingers in the garden there.

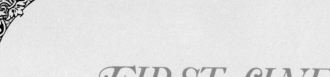

FIRST LINE INDEX

A birdie with a yellow bill 10

All night long and every night 68

All the names I know from nurse 42

As from the house your mother sees 74

At evening when the lamp is lit 41

Bring the comb and play upon it! .36

Come up here, O dusty feet! 33

Dark brown is the river 44

Down by a shining water well 18

Faster than fairies, faster than witches 21

From breakfast on through all the day 69

Great is the sun, and wide he goes 46

How do you like to go up in a swing 13

If two may read aright 66

I have a little shadow that goes in and out with me 32

In the other gardens 52

In winter I get up at night 57

I saw you toss the kites on high 12

I should like to rise and go 26

It is very nice to think 11

I woke before the morning, I was happy all the day 22

Late lies the wintry sun a-bed 58

My bed is like a little boat 40

Of speckled eggs the birdie sings 16

O it's I that am the captain of a tidy little ship 30

Over the borders, a sin without pardon 62

Summer fading, winter comes— .54

The coach is at the door at last 50

The friendly cow all red and white .48

The gardener does not love to talk .45

The lamps now glitter down the street 37

The lights from the parlor and kitchen shone out 53

The moon has a face like the clock in the hall 20

The rain is raining all around 17

The world is so full of a number of things 19

These nuts, that I keep in the back of the nest 64

The sun is not a-bed, when I 14

Three of us afloat in the meadow by the swing 24

Through all the pleasant meadow-side 49

Up into the cherry tree 25

We built a ship upon the stairs 28

What are you able to build with your blocks? 38

When children are playing alone on the green 34

Whenever the moon and stars are set 56

When I am grown to man's estate 65

When I was down beside the sea 47

When I was sick and lay a-bed 29

When the bright lamp is carried in .72

When the golden day is done 60

You too, my mother, read my rhymes 70